$9.90

EARTH SCIENCE LIBRARY
RIVERS AND LAKES
MARTYN BRAMWELL

Franklin Watts

London · New York · Toronto · Sydney

© 1986 Franklin Watts

First published in Great Britain by
Franklin Watts
12a Golden Square
London W1

First published in the USA by
Franklin Watts Inc.
387 Park Avenue South
New York, N.Y. 10016

First published in Australia by
Franklin Watts Australia
14 Mars Road
Lane Cove
NSW 2066

UK ISBN: 0 86313 450 5
US ISBN: 0-531-10262-9
Library of Congress Catalog Card
No: 86-50354

Printed in Belgium

Designed by Ben White

Picture research by Mick
Alexander

Illustrations:
Chris Forsey
Colin Newman/Linden Artists

Photographs:
Ardea 5, 6, 10r, 15r, 28t
Bruce Coleman 7, 8
Daily Telegraph Colour Library 24
Robert Esthall 29r
Fotobank 19
GeoScience Features 11
Robert Harding 15l, 20, 23, 27
Image Bank 25b
Frank Lane cover, 9, 13, 15bl, 16, 17l, 21, 22t, 26
Nick Meers 1
Tony Morrison 29l
Natural Science Photos 22b
NASA 10l
Planet Earth Pictures 4, 14br, 25t
ZEFA 17r, 18, 28b

EARTH SCIENCE LIBRARY
RIVERS AND LAKES
MARTYN BRAMWELL

Contents

The birth of a river

The life of a river can be divided into three stages. These three are usually called youthful, mature and old age. There is no sharp division between them. Just as in a human life, youth merges into maturity and then into old age. The main differences in the three stages can be seen in the shape of the river valley.

As soon as rain falls on high ground, it starts to flow downhill. At first it flows in tiny streamlets called **rills**. As the rills come together, they form mountain streams, and these eventually join lower down the slope to form a river. The small streams are called **tributaries** of the river, and the whole area drained by a river and its tributaries is called a **drainage basin**.

▽ The starting point or **headwaters** of a river high in the hills of the English Lake District. At this stage the small mountain stream has barely begun to carve itself a valley. That will come later as the stream is swelled by tributaries.

The line separating two or more drainage basins usually runs along the crest of a ridge. The ground slopes away on either side, draining away the rainwater, so the line is called a **watershed**.

In the youthful stage most of the river's energy is used to overcome the **friction**, or drag, between the water and the rocky river bed. Any energy left over is used to cut the valley deeper into the hillside. The result is that the young valley is a steep-sided V-shaped notch. As the river swings from side to side, it cuts a zigzag course, winding in and out of small headlands of high ground called **interlocking spurs**.

Soft rocks are worn away quite easily, but bands of hard rock take much longer. They form steps in the valley floor, and the river cascades over them in a series of **rapids** or waterfalls.

△ A typical youthful river in the Turkish mountains. The river winds between interlocking spurs and is fed by dozens of small tributaries draining water from the surrounding hills.

▷ No two rivers or streams are exactly alike but they are all formed by the same processes and go through the same stages. This diagram shows the main characteristics of a mountain drainage basin.

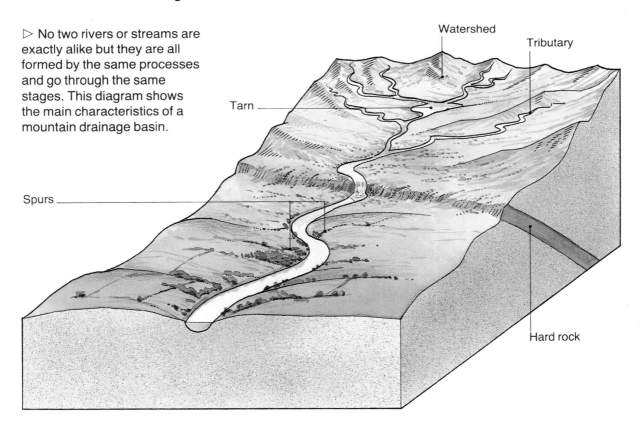

Watershed

Tributary

Tarn

Spurs

Hard rock

Deeper and wider

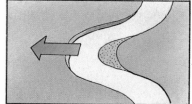

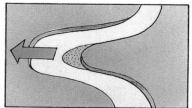

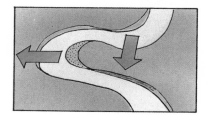

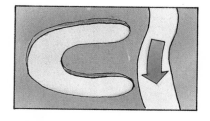

◁ The Purari River in Papua, New Guinea, is swollen by tropical rains and stained brown by the mud and silt that have been washed from the surrounding land.

When a river is at its mature stage, two important processes are at work. First the river is altering the shape of its valley. It still has to overcome friction, but there is now such a surge of water that there is plenty of energy left over for deepening and widening the river bed.

Next this process is helped by the fact that the river is now carrying along mud, sand and stones. These scrape away at the sides and bottom of the river bed. As the river swings around a bend, it wears away at the bank on the outside of the curve. It also – for the first time – drops sand and stones in the slack water on the inside. Gradually, great loops called **meanders** develop along the river's course.

By the end of this stage the river is winding along a wide, flat-bottomed valley. The spurs have been worn back, leaving straight-sided **bluffs** along the valley sides, and the broad **flood plain** is littered with the marks of old meanders.

△ This sequence of diagrams shows how a river meander develops. In the final stage the river breaks through at the narrow point, leaving a stranded **ox-bow lake**.

△ A magnificent series of meanders in the Missouri River as it crosses the dry plains of Montana. Notice how most of the trees are clustered along the river banks.

▽ In the mature stage the river meanders across a broad flat flood plain dotted with ox-bow lakes and the ridges and gravel banks of old meanders. In some rivers silt and mud are deposited after flooding. Gradually this builds up into banks called **levées**. The river may actually be above the level of its flood plain, held in by these natural barriers.

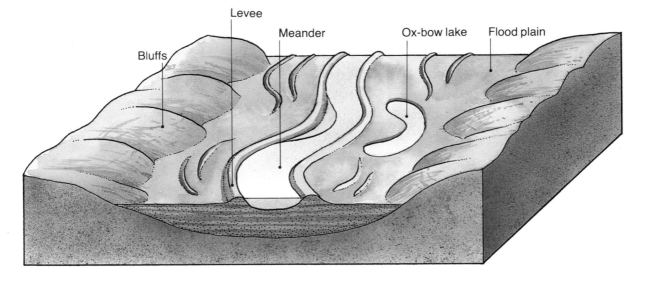

Bluffs
Levee
Meander
Ox-bow lake
Flood plain

Old man river

In old age a river enters a fascinating new habitat. The mudbanks and sandbars, salt marshes and tidal creeks of the river mouth are alternately washed by fresh water and salt.

Not all plants and animals can survive here. It is a world of specialists: of salt-tolerant plants, and the insects that live among them. Above all it is a rich feeding ground for a huge variety of birdlife. The food supply is plentiful and the birds can feed with little fear of attack by foxes, cats and weasels, who dislike the sticky mud and shifting sands.

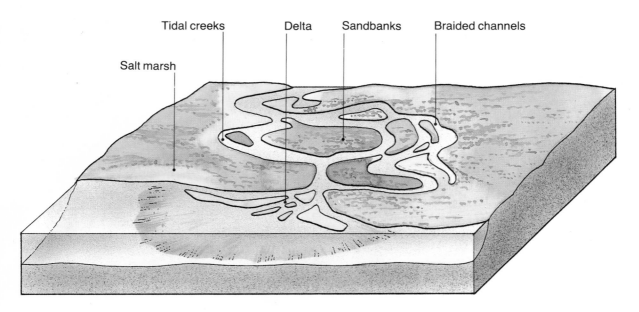

Salt marsh — Tidal creeks — Delta — Sandbanks — Braided channels

Towards the end of a river's mature stage its valley opens out. The river flows through gently sloping country between the hills, where its story began, and the sea, which will be its final destination. Its meanders become wider and wider. The valley floor is dotted with ox-bow lakes and stretches of still water in abandoned sections of river bed. The valley may now be many miles wide. The river itself may divide into several channels separated by broad areas of grassy, wooded or marshy ground.

By the time the river reaches old age, an important new process starts to play its part in shaping the river valley.

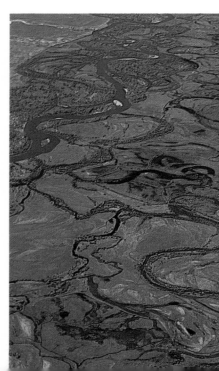

△ The heavily braided Skilak River at its junction with Lake Kenai in Alaska.

▽ The Green River in Wyoming – a mature valley almost filled with old channels and ox-bow lakes.

By this stage the river is carrying an enormous volume of water, as well as a huge load of mud and silt. But its speed has dropped. The river is now flowing over almost flat land. The powerful surge of the middle stage has now given way to a much slower, sluggish movement of the water. Instead of wearing away the sides and bed of its channel, the river is now doing just the opposite.

As its speed slows, the river can no longer carry such a heavy load and so it starts to drop sand and mud on the river bed. This process is called **deposition**. The channel gets shallower as the sandbanks and mudbanks build up, and the river gets wider and wider – often splitting up into dozens or even hundreds of channels. At this stage it is called a **braided** river, because it looks like hair that has been braided. The channels divide, rejoin, then divide again as they flow among the sand and mudbanks.

The river has now entered its final phase. Soon it will meet the sea.

Where rivers meet the sea

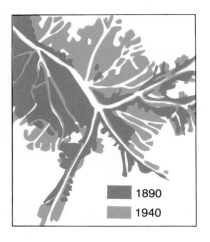

1890
1940

△ Because of its shape, the delta of the Mississippi is called a bird's-foot delta. The courses of its main channels have changed many times over the years.

Where a river meets the sea, its valley opens out into a wide stretch of open water called an **estuary**. For many miles upstream the river may be tidal – its level rising and falling as the ocean tides surge in and out of the river mouth. In some rivers, such as the Severn in England and the Seine in France, incoming tides can send a wave of water 1 m (3 ft) or more high surging up the river. Such waves are called tidal **bores**.

Most large estuaries have probably been formed by the flooding of the last few miles of a river valley – either by a rise in sea level or because the land has subsided. The channel is usually kept open by the scouring effect of the river and tides, but some deposition does occur. At low tide in the Thames estuary, for example, large areas of mudflats are exposed.

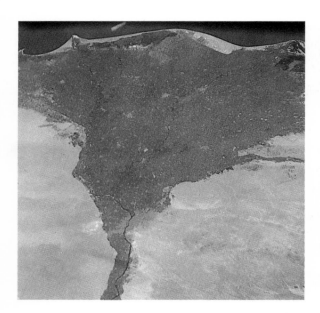

△ The huge triangular delta of the Nile stretches 160 km (100 miles) from Cairo to the coast and nearly 250 km (155 miles) from west to east.

△ Salt marsh – at the meeting of fresh water and salt – is inhabited by highly specialized animal and plant types.

Because estuaries allow ocean-going ships to unload their cargo well inland, they have always been important gateways to trading countries. Look at an atlas and see how many major cities are built on the estuaries of great rivers.

Rivers carrying large amounts of sediment often form **deltas** instead of estuaries. These are large flat areas of sand, silt and mud, crossed by countless braided outflow channels. They form where the ocean currents close to the shore are not strong enough to sweep away the sediment.

Major deltas like those of the Nile, Hwang-ho and Ganges-Brahmaputra provide some of the richest and most heavily cultivated land in the world. But they are also very vulnerable to flooding. **Monsoon** storms have often devastated the estuary of the Ganges-Brahmaputra.

△ Brant geese are just one of the many species that gather on mudflats and in tidal creeks to feed on the rich supply of food there.

11

The life of the river

▽ Life in a European fresh-water pond. The banks are clothed in wild flowers, including yellow loosestrife and marsh marigolds, while tall stems of cattail rise from the water. Beneath the surface there are snails and leeches and flatworms, and the caddis fly larva in its "house" of sand grains.

River plants and river animals naturally differ from one part of the world to another, just as the animal and plant life of any habitat varies from continent to continent. But it is only the particular species that change. The same general *types* of animals and plants are found in rivers all over the world. Each one is specialized for life in one particular "slot" or "niche" in the living system of the river.

For example, among the plants there will be some that grow in the riverbank soils. Some float on the surface of the water with their roots trailing below, while others anchor themselves to stones on the river bed.

▽ A mangrove swamp on the banks of the River Amazon. A black caiman crawls along the bank while an anaconda, one of the world's largest snakes, lurks in the water.

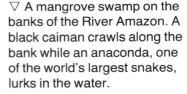

Among the animal life there will be fish that feed on algae – the microscopic primitive plants that grow on rocks or float on the surface of pools. Others sift their food from the mud on the river bed. Some fish, like salmon and pike, and the piranha of South America, are specialized hunters. They live on the smaller fish of the river. And these in turn feed on the water snails and leeches, beetles and spiders, and the larvae of the thousands of insects that lay their eggs in the water and on the stems and leaves of water plants.

Among the larger animals are fish hunters like crocodiles and alligators, otters and herons, and plant eaters as varied as the North American beaver and the African hippopotamus.

△ The otter is a powerful streamlined fish hunter. It has webbed feet, a long thick tail, and needle-sharp teeth. It can dive for up to seven minutes.

▽ River rapids in Alaska. Male and female sockeye salmon fight their way upstream to breed. The powerful male has a humped back and hooked upper jaw.

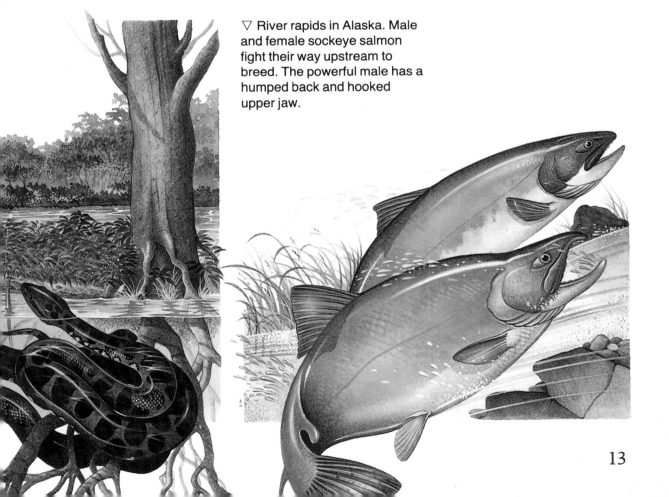

13

Nature's bloodstream

Lakes and rivers are the bloodstream of the natural world. Like the human bloodstream they carry nutrients from one part to another. Nutrients are the things that keep any living system properly fed and nourished. The most obvious nutrient is food, but just as important are oxygen and the many other chemical substances necessary for life.

Lakes and rivers perform another very important task. Just like the human bloodstream, they wash away waste material and poisons, keeping the whole system fresh and in good health. The state of a country's waterways is a good guide to the health of its wildlife.

▷ The protected forests of the Florida Everglades are home to many unusual species – from rare ferns and orchids to tree frogs, turtles, alligators and raccoons.

▽ Millions of flamingos gather to feed in the unpolluted lakes of East Africa.

▽ A large oil refinery crowds the bank of the Delaware River in Pennsylvania.

We think of water as something very ordinary. But it is actually one of the most remarkable substances in nature. More things dissolve in water than in any other liquid. This makes it an excellent carrier of nutrients. It also makes it one of the most useful of all natural materials. Water is used in many industrial processes, from cooling power stations and making steel to preparing food products.

But this ability to dissolve other substances makes it very easy to poison natural waterways. Since the start of the industrial age people have poured the waste products of their cities and industries into lakes and rivers. In less than 100 years, many rivers across Europe and America were killed off. The fish disappeared, along with the kingfishers, herons and dragonflies.

Today the picture is less gloomy. Tough anti-pollution laws and clean-up campaigns have brought fish and waterbirds back to many rivers.

△ Pollution like this cannot be overlooked. Brightly colored chemicals, foul smells, froth and scum all draw attention to the problem. Usually people will complain until action is taken. Unfortunately, many deadly pollutants are colorless and do not smell. They pose the greatest threat of all because they can easily go unnoticed.

Just how a river will behave as it travels from the hills to the lowlands depends on how much rainfall it receives. It also depends on how steep the slopes are and, most important of all, on the type of rock it is flowing over.

Some rocks, such as chalk and limestone, will dissolve in water and this gives the river some very special features. Most rocks, however, are worn away by the grit and stones swept along in the water.

Sedimentary rocks such as sandstone and shale usually wear away quite quickly. But it takes a river much longer to cut down through hard rocks. These include the tough fine-grained volcanic rocks like basalt, and rocks that have been baked and squeezed by volcanic activity.

△ Rapids on the McNeil River in Alaska provide perfect fishing grounds for a group of brown bears. The shallow waters make it easy for the bears to see their prey – the huge Pacific salmon battling their way upstream to breed in the mountain streams.

▷ The wild unpredictable waters of river rapids provide excitement and danger for the contestants in "white water" events for kayaks and canoes.

16

Where a river crosses a band of very hard rock, its behavior changes. Its slope becomes less steep because the river cannot cut down through the rock as fast. The result is that the water piles up in this section – crashing and churning through a series of rapids before pouring into the steeper river channel at the other side.

If the rock is very resistant, a waterfall may form. The softer rocks beneath the hard band are worn away quite easily, forming a deep **plunge pool**. The hard rock is left jutting out as an overhang. Every so often a section collapses into the pool, and very slowly the waterfall itself travels upstream. The magnificent Niagara Falls on the U.S./Canadian border are being worn back by 1–2 m (3–6 ft) every year.

▽ A series of rapids leads into the 50-m (165-ft) high Horseshoe Falls on the Canadian side of Niagara Gorge. In 25,000 years the falls will be worn back as far as Lake Erie. And the lake will empty!

Starting again

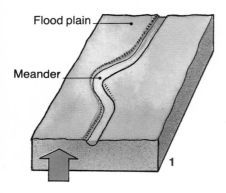

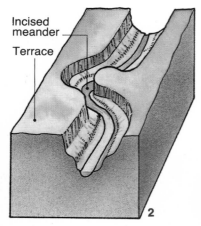

If all the landmasses stayed just as they are, and the seas and oceans remained unchanged, the world's rivers would wear away the land until there would be no hills or mountains left. The whole land surface would become one vast flat plain, crossed by meandering "old age" rivers.

But nothing remains unchanged for long in the natural world. The rocky outer layer of the earth is constantly moving and changing. The movements are far too slow for us to see, but over millions of years new mountain ranges can be pushed high into the sky. And during earth's long history, many **Ice Ages** have come and gone. At times they have locked up so much water in ice

△ **1** A mature river meanders across a flood plain.
2 If the land then rises, the river starts to cut down again as it did when it was young.

▷ The Grand Canyon of the Colorado River in the USA is a spectacular example of a rejuvenated river. The level of the "old" valley floor is picked out by the cliffs along the edge of the canyon. Over the millions of years since the land rose, the river has cut down through more than 1,900 m (6,250 ft) of sedimentary rock layers.

caps and **glaciers** that the sea level has fallen by hundreds of feet. Then the ice has melted, and the level of the seas has risen once more.

These changes alter the shapes of river valleys. If the land rises, or if the sea level falls, the river finds itself out of balance. It immediately starts cutting down through the rocks in an effort to get back to the level it was before the change. This process is called **rejuvenation**.

The mature valley we looked at earlier is broad and wide. It winds across gently sloping land, widening its valley on its journey. But if it were rejuvenated, it would immediately start cutting a deep steep-sided valley again. The remains of the old flood plain would be left high above the new valley as flat terraces called rejuvenation terraces.

▽ Many river valleys in Britain and Europe show signs of rejuvenation. The changes here were caused by a fall in sea level during the Ice Ages of the past million years. Look for the flat terrace along the left bank of the river at the foot of the steep hillside.

Underground rivers

If you look at the way towns and villages are spread over the countryside, it soon becomes obvious that many of them have close links with rivers and streams. Some will have grown up in fertile valleys fed by mountain streams. Others, especially large towns and cities, may be at the farthest point up a river that could be reached by sea-going trading ships. Some mark the widest point that could still be spanned by a bridge.

But many towns and villages owe their origins to streams and rivers flowing underground. Settlements like these are often strung out along the foot of a line of hills. They are called "spring line" settlements, and they have grown up where natural springs bring underground water to the surface.

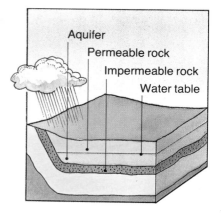

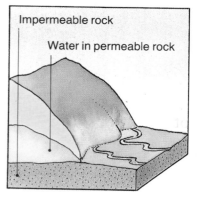

△ The top diagram shows how water is stored in underground rocks. Rainwater soaks into the tiny spaces in **permeable** rocks like sandstone. It is prevented from soaking away by **impermeable** rocks such as clay. The water-holding layer is called an **aquifer**.

The second diagram shows how springs can form at the junction between permeable and impermeable rocks. The photograph shows farmland watered by springs along the foot of the South Downs in southern England.

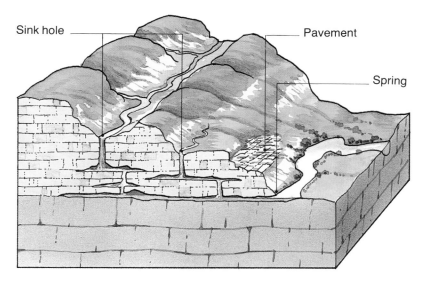

Sink hole — Pavement — Spring

◁ Typical limestone scenery is dry and barren. Most of the rainwater drains quickly into underground passages. The thin dry soil supports very little vegetation apart from short tough grasses and hardy rock plants that grow in cracks in the rock.

Limestone scenery has a character all of its own. There are valleys without streams. There are rock "pavements" of limestone blocks with deep cracks between them. There are places where streams vanish down holes in the ground, and others where streams appear just as unexpectedly from caves beneath limestone cliffs.

All this is because calcium carbonate – the main mineral in limestone – dissolves in water. As rain falls through the air, it absorbs carbon dioxide. This makes it slightly acid. And this in turn makes it even more effective in dissolving the limestone rock.

As the water trickles down through cracks in the limestone, the dissolving process widens them. Over millions of years they grow – eventually forming an underground system of passages, caves and grottoes.

But as well as dissolving the limestone, the water can use it to build fantastic sculptures. As water drips from the roof of a cave, some of the calcium carbonate is left sticking to the rock. Slowly, more and more of the mineral is added until the cave is festooned with **stalactites**.

△ Calcium carbonate from the dripping water forms into stalactites, which hang from the cave roof, and **stalagmites**, which grow up from the floor. Sometimes the two meet to form floor-to-roof pillars.

21

Drought and flood

In many parts of the world, floods and droughts are rare. Temperate regions, for example, have warm dry summers and mild wet winters. There are occasional water shortages in very dry summers. Some small-scale flooding happens in winter when rivers burst their banks or when high tides driven by storms flood low-lying coastal regions. But most years are free of extremes.

Other parts of the world are not so fortunate. Millions of people live in dry grassland and partial desert areas where there is very little rain, even in a good year. Here, drought is an ever-present threat. If there is no rain, an entire year's food may be lost. If there is no rain for several years, then millions face starvation. This is what happened across the dry region of Africa in the early 1970s and mid 1980s.

△ Even in the driest desert there is some water beneath the surface. Here, along a dry Algerian river bed, palms push their roots down to the moisture far below.

△ In many parts of India flooding is a regular and familiar part of life. The people go about their normal business as best they can. But in hard-hit country areas the loss of lives, homes and crops causes great hardship.

◁ Sun-baked earth and patches of thorn scrub are typical of the partial desert areas of Ethiopia and Sudan. If the last few plants are eaten by goats and cattle, or taken for firewood, the desert takes over completely.

Some parts of the world suffer from opposite extremes of weather. Tropical regions receive much more rain than temperate regions and it is spread throughout the year. In these regions the air is very hot and it holds a huge amount of water. The combination produces frequent thunderstorms and heavy rains. Most violent of all are the monsoon rains that sweep into India and Southeast Asia in May and June each year. The rivers cannot cope, and floods are common.

Perhaps the biggest threat in tropical regions comes from hurricanes. These huge circular storm systems may be 400 km (250 miles) across, with winds of 200 km/h (125 mph) and violent rain and hail storms. Each year they cause widespread damage in the Caribbean region, in India and Southeast Asia, in China and Japan.

Highways of trade

For thousands of years rivers have provided great civilizations with their most fertile land and with natural highways between their cities. Four thousand years ago the River Nile was the main highway of the kingdom of Egypt. Farther to the east the Tigris and Euphrates watered the fertile lowlands of Mesopotamia and linked the ancient cities of Babylon and Ur.

From the fifteenth century to the present day, explorers, adventurers, traders and missionaries have used rivers as the best way (and often the only way) to reach the interior of new lands. The Mississippi and Missouri provided routes into the heartland of southern United States. The Amazon and Orinoco led explorers into the jungles of

△ With their heads protected by lightweight "crash-hats" members of the 1968 Blue Nile Expedition fight to control their inflatable as it is swept through a wide expanse of rapids.

South America. And in Africa, such famous explorers as Mungo Park, David Livingstone and H. M. Stanley found that rivers offered the only possible routes into the heart of what was then called "The Dark Continent."

As Britain and Europe entered the industrial age in the nineteenth century, rivers again played a major role, carrying coal and iron ore, timber and farm produce. Today the Rhine is still Europe's main waterway. It rises in the Alps and flows through the great agricultural and industrial regions of Germany and Holland until it reaches the sea at Rotterdam. Strings of barges pass up and down the river carrying coal and steel, petroleum and chemicals, timber, farm goods and the factory products of Europe's trading nations.

In North America the great waterway of the St. Lawrence Seaway carries large ships as far west as Lakes Superior and Michigan. It links Chicago, Detroit, and the great farmland regions of Canada and America with the sea routes of the Atlantic.

Rivers and canals keep industrial goods on the move all over the world – from the busy waterways of Europe (below) to the sturdy tug hauling timber barges through the dark forests of Borneo (above).

Lake and river people

Millions of people throughout the world depend on lakes and rivers for their livelihood.

Inland fishermen use dozens of ingenious fish-catching methods in addition to hooks and lines, nets of all kinds, and a wide variety of traps.

The lake fishermen of Benin in West Africa use weighted circular nets which they cast over fish shoals. In Japan, trained cormorants are used to catch river and lake fish. In the flooded rice fields of Asia, people trap slow-moving fish beneath basket-work "cover pots." Some South American tribes hunt fish with poisoned arrows, or stun the fish with poisons extracted from plants. In Denmark, eels are speared through the ice of frozen lakes. The list is almost endless.

▽ A Malaysian fisherman using a hand-thrown cast-net in the shallow water at the edge of a lake. Great skill is needed to cast the net so that it lands gently and fully spread over the shoal. The net's weighted edges sink very quickly, trapping the fish.

△ The stilt-house dwellers of Thailand use the river for fishing and travel and the forest for hunting.

△ Bathing "ghats" (or steps) on the River Ganges at Varanasi in northern India. For Hindus, the Ganges is a holy river. It has many names. One of them means "The destroyer of poverty and remover of sorrow".

Some people make use of rather unusual resources of rivers and lakes. In Sri Lanka, for example, river sands are sifted for sapphires, rubies, garnets and other precious stones.

The Uru Indians of Lake Titicaca, in the Andes of Peru, live by fishing and hunting waterbirds. Their canoe-shaped boats and their houses are made from the reeds that grow in the lake. Half a world away the Ma'dan, or Marsh Arabs, also build their houses of reeds. They build them on artificial islands of reeds and mud in the lagoons between the Tigris and Euphrates rivers.

In dense rainforests, rivers are often the only means of traveling from one village to another. The Zaire River, for example, is the main artery of central Africa as it has more than 15,000 km (9,300 miles) of navigable waterways. There, and in the forests of Thailand and the Amazon, many tribes live in stilt houses along the river banks.

Water at work

Waterwheels have been in use for more than 2,000 years. Today they seem very simple, but they were the first step on the road to industrialization. Before the waterwheel, all power had come from the muscles of men, women and working animals.

The waterwheel was probably invented in the Middle East, but its use soon spread. The earliest ones were used to drive mills for grinding corn. Much later, just before steam power brought in the industrial age, water wheels were being used to power forges, pumps and weaving machines.

The days of the waterwheel are long past. But water power is still with us. **Hydroelectric** stations use the water flow of great rivers or water flowing from artificial lakes to drive huge generator turbines. The Hoover Dam, built across the Colorado River in 1936, and the Grand Coulee Dam in Washington State, finished in 1942, are two of the biggest.

△ Cenarth Mill in Wales has an "undershot" wheel. The stream was carried past the mill wall in a stone channel so that the water struck the blades as it rushed beneath the wheel.

▷ The Hoover Dam on the Nevada–Arizona border is 221 m (725 ft) high and 380 m (1,247 ft) long. Lake Mead, created by the dam, is 185 km (115 miles) long and up to 13 km (8 miles) wide. As well as supplying electricity, the dam is used for flood control and for irrigating farmland in California, Arizona and Mexico.

But the most powerful of all will be the 11 billion dollar Itaipu power station on the Parana River on the border between Brazil and Paraguay. Part of the power plant was opened in 1984 and the huge project is due for completion in 1989.

Brazil, Canada, Norway and Sweden all make at least three-quarters of their electricity by hydroelectric generators. In the future, this method will be increasingly important to many developing countries in Africa and Asia.

The other main use of water is for **irrigation** – that is, for watering land in dry regions so that it can be used to produce crops. Irrigation is an expensive process, but it is one of the main weapons in the fight against hunger and starvation in many parts of the world.

▽ Food production on the dry stony ground of the island of Malta is greatly improved by irrigation. Water held in a small storage reservoir is fed by pipes and channels to greenhouses and to small terraced fields.

◁ One of the turbine rooms in the main dam of the Itaipu power station. The finished project will have 18 turbines.

29

Glossary

Aquifer   Any rock that will hold water in it or allow water to pass through it. Aquifers act like sponges. After heavy rain, water that soaked into the ground slowly seeps into rivers.

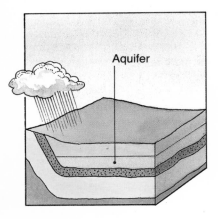

Aquifer

Bluff   A headland, hill or cliff with a very steep slope. The word is usually used for steep slopes at the sides of a valley.

Bore   A tidal wave in a river valley. A bore will develop where the ocean tide surges in to a wide estuary that then narrows into a funnel shape.

Braided   A descriptive word meaning split into many channels that keep joining, dividing and then joining again.

Delta   A broad area of mud or sand where a river empties into the sea or a lake. It forms when the sea currents are too weak to wash away the material dropped by the river.

Deposition   The laying down of silt, mud and other sediments by a river. Rivers deposit silt as their speed drops. Dripping water in limestone caves deposits calcium carbonate on the rock surfaces.

Drainage basin   The whole area of land that drains into one river system. It is separated from the next drainage basin by a watershed, usually along the top of high ground.

Estuary   The wide mouth of a river where its valley opens out at the coast.

Flood plain   The flat open valley floor of a mature river. In some cases the river may actually be *above* the level of the flood plain – held in by high banks called levées. The Mississippi River is the best-known example.

Friction   The physical force that tries to stop two things sliding over each other. Friction between water and river bed slows down the water flow. That is why the fastest flow of a river (or glacier) is always in mid-stream – well away from the banks.

Glacier   A slowly moving river of ice that flows down the side of a mountain under its own weight.

Headwaters   The small streams at the head of a river.

Hydroelectricity   Electrical energy generated using the forces of moving water in a river or flowing from a natural or man-made lake.

Ice Age   A period in the earth's past when large areas were covered with ice sheets and glaciers. In the Carboniferous Period (345–280 million years ago) ice sheets covered parts of South America, most of South Africa, all of India and the southern part of Australia – all of which were then joined together. The most recent Ice Age started about 1 million years ago and has probably not yet ended.

Impermeable   A word used to describe something that will not let water pass through it. Granite is impermeable. So is clay. Chalk and sandstone are not.

Interlocking spurs   Small headlands that jut out from the sides of the valley of a mountain stream. Looking up the valley, each spur is partly hidden by the one in front of it.

Irrigation   The artificial watering of dry lands so that crops can be grown.

Lake   An expanse of water surrounded by land. A lake may have one or several rivers flowing into it but usually has one main river flowing out. In temperate regions the amount of water flowing into the lake

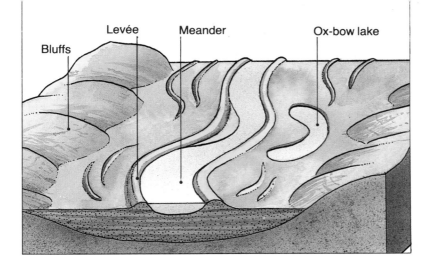

Bluffs   Levée   Meander   Ox-bow lake

usually keeps pace with that lost by outflow and evaporation, so the lake stays roughly the same size. However, if rainfall is seasonal, the lake may shrink in the dry season. Lake Chad in Africa, for example, ranges from 15,500 to 77,700 sq km (6,000–30,000 sq miles) according to the season. Lake Eyre in the Australian desert dries up completely in the dry season.

Levée   A bank built up by the deposits of mud and silt after flooding.

Meander   A wide loop in a river's course, caused by the river wearing away the bank on the outside of a curve.

Monsoon   The complicated seasonal weather systems that bring violent winds and torrential rain to parts of India and Southeast Asia.

Ox-bow lake (also called a meander cut-off).   A crescent-shaped lake formed when a meander in a river course

forms an almost complete loop. The river then breaks through the narrow neck of land to create a new, almost straight course again.

Permeable   Anything that will allow water to pass through it. Sandstone rock is permeable because water can move through the tiny spaces separating the grains.

Plunge pool   A deep pool at the foot of a waterfall, formed by the erosive power of the falling water and the stones that are swept into it and swirled around in it.

Rapids   Stretches of very turbulent water in a river. They form where the river bed suddenly steepens, where the bed is choked by rocks and boulders, or where the river flows over a band of very hard rock.

Rejuvenation   The process of "making young again". A river is said to be rejuvenated when changes in the level of the land make it behave as if it were younger than it really is.

Rill   A tiny rivulet of water, not yet big enough to be called a stream.

Sedimentary rocks   Rocks like sandstone, mudstone and chalk, formed when particles of rock material or the remains of marine animals pile up on the sea bed and later turn to rock.

Stalactites   Limestone formations that hang from the roofs of caves and tunnels. They are made of calcium carbonate deposited on the rocks by dripping water.

Stalagmites   Structures formed in exactly the same way as stalactites but on the floor of the cave.

Tarn   A small mountain lake, usually filling the bottom of a cirque or corrie – a bowl-shaped hollow scooped out of a mountain side by moving ice when the mountain was covered by glaciers.

Tributary   Any stream or river which flows into another, larger, river.

Watershed   The dividing line between two or more river drainage basins.

Index

PRINTED IN BELGIUM BY
proost
INTERNATIONAL BOOK PRODUCTION